love

song

love song

- Poems & Prose -

Cybele

Loving Life Foundation
San Luis Obispo, CA

Order this book online at **www.trafford.com**
or email orders@trafford.com

Most Trafford titles are also available at major online book retailers.

Printed in the United States of America.

ISBN: 978-1-4269-9004-5 (sc)
ISBN: 978-1-4269-9005-2 (hc)
ISBN: 978-1-4269-9006-9 (e)

Library of Congress Control Number: 2011914121

Trafford rev. 03/07/2012

 www.trafford.com

North America & International
toll-free: 1 888 232 4444 (USA & Canada)
phone: 250 383 6864 ♦ fax: 812 355 4082

To my family,
those of blood and those of soul,
my sisters, brothers, best friends,
God kids, and spirit guides.
You have each been an angel to me.
Loving you is my heaven.
We are a sacred circle.
I am so grateful.

To Mandy,
whose extraordinary spirit
inspired so many of these words.
Thank you for being you.
Our differences are a holy design.
Our love is as well.
Between hearts, there is a pathway.
Always.

To Booma,
my twin soul and teacher,
whose grace and nurturing never cease.
You will always be me and I will always be you.
Forever and even then…

And to God, my great Beloved,
my Teacher and Friend.
You are the bomb and the balm.
Thank you for this Life
and for showing up perfectly as everyone
and everything!

Out beyond ideas
of wrong-doing and right-doing,
there is a field.
I'll meet you there.

~ Jalal ad-Din Rumi

Foreword

I am so humbled and excited to be given the privilege of expressing my admiration and respect for Heidi Cybele Grant, the humanitarian, the poet, the healer, the true servant of love. I say these things with the assurance and authority of one who has lived with her as my family member for ten years. I've seen her display extraordinary courage dealing with physical illness and the criticism of those who are uneducated about the effects of Lyme disease, both mental and physical. This book is filled with the wisdom of the heart. Heidi has deliberately exposed her vulnerability and been an example of how that very vulnerability, when embraced, leads you directly to the truth – that love is all that really matters.

Cinnamon Hopkins Lofton
Spiritual Counselor
Author of Here, Now

Preface

Poetry is my way of moving energy. I have written since I was a child, mothering myself with what came through me. I was first moved to publish this compilation of inspired words at a time in my life when I made a series of choices that did not work. I had chosen not to remember the truth I've laid to paper over the years and had slipped back into a fear dance that did not become me. Partial surrender to trusting God's way is a very tricky business that I do not recommend. It never pans out to deny this Love that is inside me. During that extraordinary time of reckoning, as I rededicated myself to the discipline of devotion, my own words were there to soothe me. They were friends that called me home. May they be the same for you.

Heidi Cybele Grant
Laguna Beach, CA
February 2012

This book is a love song
to
the
God
in
you.

Let these words seduce you into your Self. Let the sound of them drum off the tongue and pick at the iceberg that now encases your heart. May they stimulate courage. Nothing can hold us back when we are no longer afraid to trust.

Lose all the notions you've held so close.
They have no meaning now.
Lose them and meet yourself in this dark.
Everything you've ever most deeply wanted
is already yours,
is with you in one form or another.
I will dance with you here,
out beyond desire.

Because there is no well, I become water.
Because the heart of this world sleeps,
I have chosen to be the awakened spirit that lives its
dream.
Instead of remaining hungry, dear one,
become the nourishment you need.

What would you be willing to do for oneness?

There are times my loved ones ask me to do things I was not designed to do. I am a heart. I cannot detox for the liver or do the heavy lifting of bones. These have to learn the joy of accomplishing such feats themselves.

I am your center, your soul muscle that works tirelessly on your behalf. I enliven you. I remind you that you are worth every effort. Recognize my importance in your life and yours in mine, and together we will become far more than a body.

My soul is a stallion waiting in the gate,
restless to give its all for you.

This wide-open and hollowed self,
a common reed,
noted for her divine music.

We are each instruments.
Lean towards God's breath.
Let the song that fills you be this empty, this full,
this free.

I have made Love my God.

Sure, there are other gods to worship.
We all know them:

Substance, jealousy, greed, distrust, deceit,
pride, nostalgia, security, omnipotence, seduction...

If you sway in their direction,
good luck with that.
I've knelt to them many times
on many occasions.

It never worked!

Such fleeting satisfaction,
such mediocre benefits.

The God I've chosen and I
kneel to each other,
divine mirrors,
ecstatic mutual servitude.

A life of service
is a life of joy;

Giving without condition,
the ultimate freedom.

Arrive inside this moment and meet yourself.

We are nothing but phantoms till we approach this table, surmise that it is safe, and sit down to eat.

This laden bounty is all fruit of the One to which we belong.

Breath is Her gift.

Unwrap its treasure.

Inhale and experience the gratitude
that is resident to your heart.

How patiently she sits, awaiting visitors.

How attentively she watches the door,
listens for any sound, awaiting you.

If this is slumber, don't wake me. I want to be a moth to this flame. There are flashes of lightning in my heart that the ground in me swells to meet. It is a total annihilation welcomed with every cell. Waves of passion overtake me. The eyes close and the head tips back to greet them. It is the sacred dance of homecoming, the new blending itself into old in the ritual manner and all the curtains opened wild and wide to the wind in utter surrender, speaking the words, move me, move me with this love you feel. Touch me like I want only you, only you to do. I am here, yours, present and ripe, with utter and raw abandon.

Let love feed the deep hunger. Let love finally salve and heal the wounds you say it created. God will never make a mess. Only that which isn't love topples this milk carton. Love in her richness bends to lend a hand. There is always a door home though we must decide to walk through it.

You are here to help me awaken. I am so grateful. I see that every act on your part no matter how kind or cruel is a conspiracy, at times unbeknownst to even you, that invites me, calls me to love myself no matter what. You come with God's voice and God's listening to what my soul needs. You know me psychically, implicitly. You know past knowing. The medicine you are, without understanding, without intention, is always the perfect gift. Thank you.

Reconnection with your soul requires my surrender. It takes silently stopping, pausing even breath, to gather the internal forces I've allowed to stray in divergent directions. I invite their reverberation back into this moment where you have left yourself behind. To embrace this reality of whom you've chosen to be, this other, this non-existent self, is to claim my greatest strength and breathe in life's most excruciating pain. To live here in this Presence, this peace, with or without you, is to love you unconditionally. Thank you for having abandoned Love, an excellent, perfect choice. It has been a tremendous gift, my most challenging opportunity yet. I am here, resting, breathing, unwilling to worry or mourn. I refuse to take your absence seriously. You will return eventually as we all do. Not because we must. It is simply who we are. When this game of choice ends, we relax back into the Self. Patience finds its purpose and its reward in this ultimate homecoming. All paths lead back to the One we are. For now, swing it however you like. Go wild, mosey, meander, even lose yourself deep inside the mind if you wish. Diverge and digress! Explore the sacred choice. God will ring the bell that calls your soul home in perfect time and at a pitch you are promised not to miss.

I perch sleepless and watchful, awaiting my own willingness to show up, a straggler at tonight's affair. I watch for it to resurrect itself and burn off the fear I've let settle around my heart. I'll wait up all night if I have to for the real me to arrive all fresh with evening's air and light with God's twinkled laughter that glints in my knowing eyes. I so dislike this experience of longing for the God that has always, as now, offered Herself to me in the same moment I opt for self-deception and pine for Her. It is a bleak game that spirals in a sloppy misguided fashion. No longer myself, I disconnect so that I can reemerge somehow different, melt down into a more humble version of myself. Why do I listen to that other inner self and take on her notions that bring her to a wall and keep her there? Why do we humans so often make choices that we know won't work? At the core is a mental refusal to love ourselves, to know ourselves as enough, a conundrum that shapes our lives and our world. Meanwhile, birds are conversing loudly about their daily doings, entirely aware of and totally undeterred by global warming. Meanwhile, grasshoppers groom their insect wings and don't consider being falcons. They don't contemplate going airborne. They just do.

No one has morning breath like a river.
It smells of mountains and many miles.
It is betrothed to the willows and riparian
                    flowers.
Let the mind become oxygenated.
Let it move and meander in Love's gravity.

I will devote myself to you for the rest of my life, no matter the form. The God in you is the one I worship. Your body lays itself across my mind, under mental fingers that yearn to soothe. I want to be that one to caress the quiet hours with you so close that you are my breathing, that the tide inside me has swells that you originate. Utter stillness is the love I have for you and I want it for only us, only our silent pull into each other when it is you and I and this oneness in the early hours, slumbering in God's tremendous cradle.

We see ourselves as such fragile beings and in our perceived fragility we can turn so vicious. We will only put down our daggers when we tap into our true grounding and get in touch with God's invincibility through the practice of self-love.

We come to know God through self-love.

You come to me in shapes of sorrow, the love you would not claim draped carelessly to the side. Would it take so much that you would not bring yourself to release all the dread, to strip the clothes of uncertainty and bare thin skin of marvelous, vulnerable truth, beauty beyond all other? Would you really deny what is yours? You are a beauty hidden in shrouds of guilt and shame. My love for you remains, unflinching and unclaimed.

Separation is the dream. We will never be separated, you and I. Not by the myriad tales of your mind, not by the winds that blow miles between us, not by life's epic lessons that are at times excruciating. I am here, one with you. Always. All else is illusion.

God is a wind that rushes through my heart.

I release it as it arrives in me and send it out into the world stamped with my signature.

God is a letter written in my own sacred love for you.

The blessing and the curse of it is
that the game is rigged!
There is NOTHING you can do to get God
in me
to stop loving you.

Beauty rings with the voice of a thousand
                    different bells
           sounding outside my morning window,
                reverberating from within.
It wafts over me,
            singing in the faces of the day.
Even here in this small café,
            chords are being played.
Some swim in this music,
            their movement in synch with the tides
                    of the moment.
Others sleep through the symphony of
            their own making,
        unaware of the joy that calls to them.
Most distract themselves with what isn't
            to so great an extent that it deafens
                    them.
These are the saddest I've seen.
Friend, listen…
It's been a long time, yes.
Do you remember how to trust?
It is as simple as turning toward the music.
Each new interaction is your complement.
                    Harmonize.
May we each become the masters
            of our own songs.
Take hold of this instrument that you are.
        Play its rhythm with all your might.

Few in today's world
know the experience of gardener and soil.
Often, these two
are no longer in harmony.
What is your garden like?
Have you acknowledged its depth,
evoking green buds and gods of life?
Keep tilling.
It will ripen
and become sustainable enough
to cultivate you in return.
It is the primal home,
the house of resurrection.
I speak from here,
the earthy hummus,
the dark origin of things.
God is my gardener.
She turns me over
and exposes innards to Light.
She digs holes and plants seeds.
She hallows weeded areas
and fills me with fertility.
Lusciousness I am becoming
and could not be without Her.
She dwells in me,
nurturing such a space,
it will be able to feed sizable worlds,
and leave layers and layers of livable love.

Here I sit atop this tree that sways and takes its root inside of me. I came up from soil and spirit mixed. Thank God to be neither only one nor only the other.

You who invite my eyes to lift
        themselves continually beyond their
                own
                horizons,
you who are the reflected pools
        of green that are a shifting sea inside
                me,
you've taken my heart like a
        brave white bird into your hands, raised
                them up to the world and
                        opening
                them gently,
                        wistfully,
                                and then
                                with
                                definitive grace,
                                set
                                me free.

29

I say I am available and I am. And then a wind picks up and rattles me and I claim to be distracted. I say I am distracted and I am. And then someone questions me and I let the doubt surface. I say I am afraid and I am. Fear becomes me and I claim to be drowning. Am I? All there is to do is surrender. To doubt no longer, distract no more. To love whom I love when I love and say so out loud when it serves and be still when it doesn't. The only dialogue to have is Love. Love of the God, love of the Self, love of the Us, living in me.

Our bodies are
        beasts untamed.
They lash out yet
        long so to be
                loved.
The hunter strikes
        hungry for oneness
                yet looking for meat.
Feed upon me, those that are lost.
Have your fill.
May all that I am
        remind you
                of all that you are:
Pure divinity as yet
        unspoken.
Tame the sorrow.
        Love it and speak.

Wow. Sometimes it is so hard to trust Love.
Sometimes, it just looks like the craziest business ever.

Would you tell a butterfly to emerge from its cocoon
before its time?

Be tender with the ones curled into themselves.
They are either healing or are refusing to.

You are the dream I love. You are the dream I wake to. You are the dream I live. I breathe you into me and feel the humility in me bow itself down to the ground and kiss our shared feet. The earth is the treasure that raised us up. We resemble our tender mother whom we do not worship and who continues to serve us anyway. You are that goddess nurturer, the one that brings plates of dates and seeds and fills my cup with blessed ecstasies and intricacies of being that are a complex array of beauties for me to admire, admire the rest of my beloved days. May you no longer refuse to greet Her, to know your earthy side, to embrace the one who is the curve to your hip, the roundness of lip, the one that looks exactly like my love because she is. She is dirt and rhizome and she is juice and ferment. She is the hunter, the forager. She is the lost lover hungry for splendor's touch. She's the wild glance, the tear, and the hand that knows exactly how to convey the most unspeakable gift, the ultimate need, the enduring desire, the love so great it turned itself into form so that it could sing its own name and experience its own song.

I want to start a conversation with you about God that never ends. I want my words to be as lips upon your ears that have been so hungry for a mouth to say just the right thing in that particular tone that soothes the oldest hurts. I want our topics to shape themselves the way your chest dips inward toward bone and lays your heart out so near the surface, exposed and remarkable. In this exchange, breathing you into me is common currency. It's my plentitude. It's my splendor. And in this conversation, your body unfolds and steeps itself in me like a warm and quiet bath at dusk. And when we are tired and seeking rest, stillness will take up the dialogue for us, singing God's favorite melodies to us as we sleep.

Sometimes from the mind's perspective, there isn't enough love to go around. We either give love to others at the sacrifice of ourselves, or we make others "pay" for our self-involvement.

There is another way of experiencing this issue that takes care of everyone:

What works best for one of us spiritually ALWAYS works best for the whole. And vice versa.

In this way, everyone is taught the key to joy: that giving and receiving from love are interchangeable facets of the same jewel.

Throw away shame. No pattern can be truly broken with shame as its motivating force. You will suppress perhaps, but never heal. Love is the Great Alchemist. Where shame is a fire that destroys, Love is a fire that resurrects. Breathe and release the grip of self-hatred in one hand, unworthiness in the other. Feel what it is like to trust that you are always worthy and always lovable.

Evil does not exist, only the illusion of evil. The mirage made real by our minds is a choice made by each individual to experience his or her life without Love. It does not have inherent power. It has only the power we each give to it. We can release from this "only human" perspective at any moment just as darkness must always give way to Light. Live with Love or without Love. Both actions have their reactions. That is the game of life: To love or to fear and to reap the harvest of either.

There is a 'you' that spins webs of angst and catches fears inside it to consume when hungry later. And there is a 'you' that picks up the fabric of this human experience with both hands, unravels it into divine thread, and weaves it back together, a blanket of soul that enwraps this world and heals it. Which you would you rather be?

You are the night that encompasses and you are a
new wilderness for me. I am exhilarated, then afraid,
then flying. I long for you and then retreat. You are
the unknown that is so veiled that I can stare and stare
into it and cannot adjust my sight to see what comes
next for us. We are the love that carves away until it
finds itself deep inside rock and bone and a brave
willingness to stretch inside the heart.

No addiction is worth the loss of us.
The current that takes me to you is release,
a letting go of my illusion that you are
gone from me,
that I could somehow be absent
from this magic that we together are.
Nothing can keep me from this,
the reality of merging.
All else is an intentional forgetfulness,
a pretense that is the centerpiece of
suffering.

Don't take scraps from Love when it is offering you
SO much more.

Want to become invincible?
Then be vulnerable.

One person's crisis is another person's walk in the park. It is always a matter of perspective.

Tricks of the mind are a perfect reason to start tricking your mind instead by remembering that life is all about perception.

The way our minds are wired defines our experience. Reprogram when necessary.

Release yourself from rigidity, all of your self-imposed rules that leave you raw and miserable and so unnecessarily alone.

Slip out the side.

Open the windows of your mind and let your spirit expand into the All.

In what way do you remind yourself that you are more than a body?

In what way do you remind yourself that you are more than a mind?

We suffer needlessly when we don't take time everyday to remember that we are much more than human.

Experience your spirit
or fear will have to be your default.

Oh flesh of my flesh,
        we are the earthen bone of God.
We are the throbbing heart of humanity.
The dirt of stars,
                particles of love,
        whirling in the current of the One.
How bizarre that we so often weep when
        we swim even now in such wonder,
                such complete and utter joy!
Take up all your tears, Love,
        and bet them all on freedom.
Watch yourself be lifted up and swept within.
Now is the trustworthy medium of
                resurrection.
Welcome home to this here experience
                of imploding
        into the God that we are.

I immerse myself into the Soul of all things, the common bath, and breathe from this place. I exist nowhere else any longer but HERE.

I sit in the center where there is no line of a horizon. There is no horizon or lack of one.

A Footnote to Accounting

The legacy of our beloved country:
Innocents warring innocents,
the numbers weighing lives as costs,
money always the golden benefit,
the divine rule.
There is another way.
No number, no mindset can touch it.
No value can quantify the heart
and its offering of forgiveness,
its desire to let go and begin again.
It starts here,
with the breath.

We will continue to wage war inside ourselves, against each other, and across the world, so long as we believe that peace depends on <u>anyone</u> or <u>anything</u> outside of ourselves.

When I gaze into the pure Self of you, child, I come into the landscape of my own heart that is most vibrant, most fresh. The effect is a healing. It is my own love that I gaze across and into when you take my face in your hands and smile with winks in the corners of your mouth and a voice that rings irreverent and utterly unclouded. You speak the soul of me and I sing the song of you and together we are one complete breath. Thank you.

"Look at this, Heids! What a disaster!" she said to me, her little face bright with creation as she lifted to my eyes a blackened rainbow smattered with crosses and blotches of dark paint. And then her laughter came and poured itself all over me and I was washed in a lightness of being.

Every day you breathe,
you water my faith in God.
You lift me above my reckonings,
my absolutions.
Loving you has broken my existence into pieces.
I lay down in the center of this madness
and know peace.
I know you.
No fear that raps and taps and wants to enter will
dissuade me from what I know
deepest down.

God's timing is etched on your soul.
I sit back with a witch's calm
    to witness Love's emergence
        from your depths,
            to watch as you unfold your most
                sacred passions & discover their
                    purity & their peace.
The courage to surrender to your most radiant
                    & uninhibited heart
        is quietly & assuredly growing inside you.

53

Your sunlight is sometimes
        sequestered in cloud cover.
Sometimes anger, sometimes
                hatred
            are the violent storms.
Blackness turned inward
        creates dramatic
                    thunderheads.
When this bright world
        that is my life
            is no longer blessed, no
                    longer fed by the sun
                        that you are,
I will begin to believe
        that clouds can mean
            something about the value
                of an entire star.
In the meantime,
        on this day of rains,
            I keep my vigil, sing sun songs,
                my heart ablaze.

A thick
    volcanic
        crust
    layers the
channel through
which your
    light seeps
        up & out
        into this
            bright
                world.
Take a chisel
    to that stone.
If you think
    you've tasted
    the blue magic
        of your own
            eyes already,
wait until you've made their source
        that deepest well within.
Those eyes will know the world
                as their Beloved.   They
                        will
                    teach
                    Divine
                    Grace.

If the cost for loving you is to experience
your unrest within me,
if the cost means being manhandled
by your tidal emotions,
I will bare these like a rich man:
with money to spare.
No cost is too great
to win you back from the fear that
wraps itself around you and
leaves you cold and seemingly alone
too many warm nights.
God has given me the infinite wealth I need:
The patience to wait
until you love yourself enough
to give and receive
that much.

My love, there are so many ways that my heart longs to know you. What are you like when your soul is in mid-flight? What are you like deep in the rock bed of your nature? What sings to your truest tune? I ask and the answers are in me already known. We are of one core. What words though, Love, can I embody for you, for us, that will bring you lasting peace? Only the song that longs to be sung by both together, only the song that wants to linger daily in the quiet knowing, the iron bond, the steel of trust laid down, the song that whispers its earthy overtones to our child and nourishes her, the one that worships the God in us. This is the one for me.

God,
you have bludgeoned my eyes.
I no longer see.
I grope along the walls of my life and find them
unfamiliar.
Left has become right.
Up is down.
And I've come to sit down, spinning.
God,
you have filled this heart with a love
that belongs to the unavailable.

And when there are no more tears to cry,
You are all I have left inside of me.

I am still very strongly in hibernation mode. I am so quiet outside. My gestures are slow and still, my voice withdrawn, dispassionate, detached…

All of this is a racket. There is the chemical condition of the body, yes. And then there is what I do with it, how I respond, and that is SO influential of how I BE in the world. How I choose to relate to my illness is 99.9% of the picture, no matter what my physical condition is in a moment. I see that I love the drama of sluggishness, the drug of apathy, the slipping into a daze, a quite successful sedative attempt on my senses and experiences. It is a subtle form of protection from pain. I'm willing to give up the vividness of my experiences in order to blunt any sudden emotional jabs, aches, discomforts. It's a lazy man's spirituality. Rather than reprogram to wake up, I'm reinforcing my slip-slide into oblivion. Right now, it's working for me. What will be the catalyst for my evolution away from this dull mode? The answer is an uncomfortable one in that it is far closer than my mind wants to admit. The answer lies right now beneath the game, awake and waiting in my deepest layer.

Time to get so real, so cleansed of fear,
it has no room to enter.
I shall not hold a place for it at my table.

Fear is so seductive. "Let's not grow," it whispers. "Let's hide away and rest." The seductress pounces inevitably. It has to strike. That's what fear does. It ends up at the throat. Love is patient and kind and endures. It self-sustains. Get behind me, Satan. Be in the past where I no longer dilly-dally, linger.

Temptation, sit beside me.
You are mine to love and tame and give thanks.
My teacher, my tester, my friend.

Right now, I am a love seedling. Bull, I'm a sapling! I'm strong and I can handle whatever life asks of me.

The only way to see ourselves as who we truly are is to take off the glasses of society and see ourselves through God's eyes.

How sweet the numbness we create with our favorite substances, alcohol, weed, opium, adderall, percocet, nicotine, sugar, sex... ah, the myriad blessed options to choose from! Their effects so adequate to the task of sedating the parts of our minds we hate, we forget their poisons. We rationalize and popularize their use. We say we can live without them. Our defenses rise when others warn of addiction. Meanwhile, we covet our beloved chemical mistresses that seem to lift us from ourselves. Slowly, we disconnect from our essence, becoming people we otherwise wouldn't recognize. Meanwhile, we swear this isn't happening. Only tiring of the backlash from these seductive characters will pivot us, ripen us for something new. Freeing our minds from their self-inflicting thoughts without chemical aid takes faith in our ability to do so. It takes slipping out the side of the mental barricades we've built up to be so strong. This is the inner revolution: experiencing, sometimes for the first time in many years, a lack of need for what we think of as chemical salvation. Until then, we live lives of indentured servitude. When will you tire of this self-imposed slavery? Surprise yourself. Make it now. Show yourself the limitlessness of your possibility, the flawlessness of your ability. Non-violently, revolt. Free yourself of the world's sedatives. Become your whole and complete, extraordinary self again. Reacquaint yourself with the elixir of feeling.

If you believe that Love isn't enough,
then it won't be.
Love takes trust to activate its powers.

Every life is a self-fulfilling prophecy.

How brilliant that God
chose
to make us all One,
Mirrors and Creators
of our own experience
with the power to be truthful
or
to breathe life into illusion,
the illusion of Other.

We are the cosmic joke: the divinity that questions itself, demanding proof of its own authenticity. The doubting self is never satisfied. The loving self gets all the praise through Self-assurance it could possibly need.

Worry dips into principal.

It offers no returns.

What a poor investment!

My love is your undoing.
There is no act of yours adept enough
to veil
the rough tenderness you wear.
It is uniquely yours.
It looks like fire pulled tightly
under control,
hidden under ball caps.
Still, everyone knows
the redness that you are.
'Friends.' 'Sisters.' 'Compadres.'
Perhaps we are none of these.
Perhaps we are just together
walking down this hectic moment.
We are for each other
the support every person longs for and
few provide.
It is just this:
You are worth the surrender of my every doubt.
You are the first and last reason
that I give myself to God.

We are so special
as we sit like little girls,
glowing and gabbing,
sharing breath.
It is always this way between you and I.
God collects like sediment in the corners of our
mouths,
as the love flows,
a vast river meandering through us.

Thank you, God, for making my skin so tender,
that these hands can reach out and feel
the Soul.
Thank you, God, for making my heart so open
that it can contain it All.

Come Friend,
        sit with me in the center of this stillness.
May we know our Selves no longer as our
        selves.
Instead, we are one shared cup
        brimming with God's nectar
        where the world can come to sip
        tenderly and remember itself.

More often than not, we think life's dealt us a poor hand; meanwhile we aren't making a good hand from what we've been given.

So much wishing for life to be different, for God to give us something else to make things better...

What are we willing to do for ourselves? What sweetness are we willing to concoct to enhance the day for ourselves, for others?

God is in us, waiting, untapped.

God is a tugboat that will pull any barge across a vast sea and not wish to be doing anything different.

The landscape is changing. Notice the backwaters, the canyons. Fog. Notice the newness, uncharted sensations, places where breath has not yet entered...

What we call loss is a gateway.

I stand tall here in the winter of my life.
Loss like I have never known. A deadening of ways
I've embraced so long. Fear on all sides. Does it
encroach? No. It is my own creation. I raise hands to
its insolence. I will live out this winter's gloom and
know the buds of spring. I will have made fear my
friend, the darker half that has its place as loved and
no longer heeded. All it ever wanted was to be heard
and loved in spite of itself.

There is a quiet that
settles itself around my thoughts of you
and impregnates them with
magic.
I have let desire go,
nor am I looking for distraction in your eyes.
I have tasted that wine of bitterness
enough times to let the impulse go.
I want only God in all
of its raw nature. I want
potent honesty,
stark and liberating to wash me of any remaining
doubt
and uncover my devotion
that is becoming so absolutely clear.

When love wells up in me, it burns off all mist, thought forms that cloud my vision. No place to rest this fear for even a moment before venturing onward. There are no sides to this fountain. No boundaries to cling to. Best to free up the burdens by letting them or any longings for shore go. Best at this point to float in this endless now.

Carry neither pity nor blame.
There is nothing to harbor here,
          nothing to protect
except the long shadows from a day
          that is passed.
I am no longer that child
          hiding there in the growing dark,
                    hoping to be missed.
I am no longer that little one whose innocence
          was shrouded long ago.
I am not that one who thrashed at herself, who
          wildly sought to unravel the
                    schizophrenia,
          to feign sweetness,
          to wash away the demon she was
                    deep down.
She is a phantom now, a twilight mirage.
In a moment, I am this rush of life, this angel,
          opening arms and wings to a woman
                    grown.
I rock this woman gently, this wizened child.
She, in turn,
          leaning toward sunrise,
                              rocks the world.

Someone has untethered the rope. I am set adrift upon a directionless sea. No land, no landmarks in sight. I thought that I myself was an ocean until I was taken by your tide. Now I know that I am a droplet in this vast and starry sky, this limitless world, this divine embrace. I look everywhere. No sign of you. I close eyes to this world and your light wells up inside me. We are the ebb and flow. We are this song of Love, this you, this I.

Every night, I get into a hot bath and make some one-note sounds using the fullest capacity of my breath. It is a simple act. It is the first seat violin, striking a note to which the myriad cells of my being can then tune. It is the foghorn that radiates out to the furthest reaches of my universe with its call for cooperation.

I have spent my lifetime getting to know myself
and I have come to the conclusion that I love her.
I see the world reflected in her eyes.

Family. My body is hewn with this thread. It takes on the shape of my most cherished self: you, the collective love, defining it. I am fine muslin draped in surrender across a substance known for its shameless and elegant togetherness. I am the cloth that dreams itself this body. In visions, our rough-cut form is taken up by Mercy's hand and tenderly worked into quelled and perfect honesty more sacred than any rare or beloved stone. May this human circle immerse so deeply into its own spirit self that it gets lost in its own rich dream, venturing away from its fearful and limiting notions of itself, never to return. Kinship cleansed of doubt will be the hearty seed buried deep and sure for future generations. It will embed into soil and flesh, and father the sprouted messengers of healing we came to experience ourselves as being. Life's most empowered living and breathing song is the trust we raise up with one collective hand in thanks to the creators we are and to the One All that is the sacred blending possible.

The wind that picked up last night swept out all remaining traces of dust and doubt. The result is a vivid inner dawning that greets the morning as it's own. I rise gleaming from my bed, tones from my body emerging in pronounced and unspoken harmony. Smiles perch on my lips like kids seeking excuses to burst out and flower into themselves. I am so empty. My soul has space to stretch and breathe deep and move around. She ambles about the place, delighted. Purity of being like this is worth every decision it takes, every perfect motion that love incites to be here.

My purpose is a spiritual one.
My body is the temple.
My heart knows the flowers
and of what they speak.
Our lives are fragile things,
blossoms in the riverbed,
circling mesmerized in still pools,
not knowing what comes with the flood
that may someday rise and pummel us.
The washing may or may not deliver us.
It may or may not come at all.
Blossoms floating quietly in placid pools
don't worry.
Neither will I.

A mountain explodes and a lake wells up in the crater that remains. What an artist is this Nature Being, the God inside this world. I know my heart lives both in and far beyond this body. It meets itself where white snow and cloud interface with elevated rock and the bluest water speaks of sky. So crisp, so solitary, sculpting silence into sound, light into form, love into these words that I now come to know and playfully pretend are my own. More and more these days, I open my mouth and to my surprise it is God that speaks, announcing joy, first to me, then to this precious world and anyone in it who will listen.

I sip forever with you. I close my eyes and taste the vastness of now. A spacious void exists between where I end and you begin. Then the voice from within, the one that knows my every breath, feeds itself to me slowly and I know myself as the Friend, the one that resounds inside you every time you opt to lean courageously in the direction of love.

I know you could argue the point.
What is the point of that?
I have no need to be right or wrong.
I have no need for nostalgic words.
Why disconnect now?
Why sugarcoat something already
        so ripened, whole?
You spread yourself out in my direction.
I'm all poised attention.
Undress and lay me out
        as sensuously as you do yourself.
Let this love that harbors no
        illusion unwind and weave us
                into one pattern,
        tightly hewn tapestry of sighs ,
so that we no longer know the miles as
                breadth.
We now know only depth.
No doubt remains. We are the same.
Beloved.

There are so
        many voices
                inside you, Angel.
I've leaned in close to
        listen to each of
                them.
Together, they are a
        cacophony of
                sound.
I've been lost inside that
        ruckus for a time.
I will stick from now on to
        the one that keeps the latest vigil.
I will put my blindfold back
                on and stay up
        nights with the one that sings
                to me her most
        sacred and fearless songs.
The harmony we create is perfect.
        This is why we stay up late, She and I,
                past reckoning hours to sing,
                        sing our
                                heart's desires.
        Let Her be, Love.
        Silence all other voices.
                        She is the one,
                                most brilliant
                                You.

There is an emptiness I feel when I seek to touch this that we are together. It is formless in a way my mind cannot reach. This is a love that slips through the fingers that tighten. It is a love that will know itself only in the letting go. Mist meets itself fleetingly and then becomes pure light. As in all of its truest forms, love requires complete release. I stretch myself across this life and await the dissolution. Any time now...

Sometimes,
      I am the cup that contains you.
You intoxicate me.
I want my desires to smart
      so that I am left branded with a constant
            reminder of what can and can't be.
The answer is to become an ascending spiral of
                oneness.
I reach out to places in you that haven't been
                known,
      hoping to heal the ancient wound
            that sometimes has you.
I am a cup that contains you.

Story builder, what pieces and parts of life will you construct with next? Ones of chaotic bravery, a grand distain, self-deception that is wired down and in so deep that it looks like truth? Why settle for the tragic or cruel? If you insist on always having a victim, you will have to cast a villain time and time again. Let your next vision be the grain that is already separated from its chaff, clean and gleaming, ready for use. Let it be a sun that lights up your life from the inside. Make it about only you. Be sure this time that it's the story you most deeply care to live.

Where I am the soul,
you are the earth into which I root and make my
stand.
Where you are the Grace,
I am the wind that unfurls your sail casting you upon
God's sea.
Where one is, the other must be.
It is God's cosmic joke,
this 2-in-1 geometry.

Together,
we have approached God's alter.
            Two petals.
We have laid ourselves delicately down upon Her
Humble Majesty
            in total awe,
                        just being.

Your mouth and your eyes
        work against each other.
They no longer harmonize.
It's so tempting to listen to
        your lack of feeling
            & believe.
Sweetheart,
        we have been the shadow light of stars,
            the ones that give and the ones that receive
                the bounty of the Spirit world.
I will continue to walk this edge.
I will be the one to stand in light
        and simultaneously
            cast a shadow.

Life is full of tragedy. Turn that garment inside out. The inner lining is perfect bliss. One does not come without the opportunity to create the other. Either way. It's up to you.

Realizing this is wisdom.
Exercising it is enlightenment.

When I touch you, Little Bird,
vast winds lift you to my lips.
You taste of God,
a nectar so rich and lasting,
a feast for all the souls that are.
Fragile one,
how wondrous that,
so slight of frame,
you fill my eyes
with Light
and laughter that speaks
Our Name.

Your love is the richest I've ever known.
Blackest soil for every seed I long to sprout.

I am moving away from fear now while even this very morning I was moving toward it. I so dig that it doesn't take a process. It takes what it takes to heal through willingness. Willingness determines timing. It shapes everything. Inner alchemy. I have created my peace again.

I have entered the realm of magic that is accessible to everyone: the remarkable choice to be grateful, even and especially for the parts of life I don't like.

Nothing speaks to me like this living moment
that breathes between us
and sips at the nectar that we are.
This gift
drips from an eternal spring,
effortless
and with no end.
No words, Sweetness, can touch the Quiet
that we have invited
to wrap itself around us with its
gentle knowing.
No thought can touch this robe,
no matter how reverent or sincere.
All analysis is laid down.
All doubt and lack of doubt dissolve in this beingness.
We enter the river where all is fed and the mind
finally has a home.
In this way, together,
we rest.

Navigation over a sleeping dog
        involves lifting skirt and child
                simultaneously.
Comfort is a substantive grip,
        bringing baby to breast,
                a clarity that does not hesitate.
And every day is the same:
        a glance that redirects,
                a touch that can stir up
                        the courage of a child.
The knack of a mother is in discovering
        her way to self-sustain.
Her tears and laughter are like none other.
So potent, a mother's breath
        creates and influences whole realities
                simply and by itself.
She swings love on hips.
She drips life from her breasts.
Her boundless knowing is the presence that
                soothes
        at every beginning and each end
                of rivers called days and years.
Life in two seedlings is growing
        and mother is blessed
                by who she is becoming.

Right and wrong connote good and bad. Every being is innately loving no matter how unkind their actions. We do "wrong" when we believe that we are wrong. Avoid calling yourself wrong. Ever. It will perpetuate fearful behavior. Look to your innocence first and decide now to do differently that which doesn't work in your life.

Funny how much we fight having to take responsibility for our experiences of life when the reward for doing so is always joy.

I must admit that sometimes my mind wishes that God had not shown me your divine magnificence so that I would not have become so stricken at it's absence. I miss who you really are so very much. I obsess on rediscovering/uncovering her. The right words. An explosive argument that finally unravels this mask you wear. A night of passion from which you get so lost that fear is never a kingdom you can return to again. I feel as though I will not live without you well. It is a distractive and destructive thought form of which I must rid myself. You cannot save me. Not even with your best self. I teeter on a chasm of my own devising. I grow sicker everyday believing I cannot live without your love. Healing will come in realizing that I will never have to.

Us-ness is the dessert
following the main course meal:

Surrender, rain or shine.

To help us break free of addiction,
God is liable to do anything.

Be brave with me, my love.

If I impart anything to this world, let it be that life is downright magical. Crazy. And glorious.

Free yourself. Put every ounce of energy, every cell of your body into it.

Do it orgasmically.

Forget formalities.
Let's cut straight to the vulnerable part.

We are all in this way tempted:
How, in short order, we let Love
        become not enough.
The details storm in,
        rational raiders of our own making.
Legitimacy is a rock wall of erected doubt.
The calluses thicken against these thought stones.
Inspiration aside, laughter dwindled,
        we lick wounds
                and point away from ourselves
                        at supposed aggressors,
        all the while, the knowing
                gleaming in our eyes.
Such a strange mirage we tend to make of this
        human twilight, this forgetfulness of our
                power to choose and live in
                        the God,
                                the Love,
                that we long to, that we came to
                        be.
No fear can survive Love's surety.
No Love will seek to overpower a chosen doubt.
We are faced with the present question always:
        Which will it be?

How can you say there is no choice?
Even as you speak,
        you choose to be here. There are plenty of exit
strategies, none of which you have
        implemented.
So, since you've decided to hang out, why not relax
        into your now?
Why believe in later?

Sister,
we are of the same womb,
mixed together by blood and Spirit.
My love for you is a child that I give birth to.
We are varied colors of the One,
the same sunlight casting its new face across each
moment.
Sister,
Look carefully. I arise in you.
It is only our reflections in the mirror that are
different.
You are my mother, my
daughter.
I am you pretending to be me.
Sister,
you hide yourself from me.
Find me within.

What is it that will melt the sadness and hardness around our hearts and inspire the love deep within to rise and sing?

The simple sound of 'Yes.'

God uses this in-love business to stir the pot, to raise the bar on our willingness to burn off our shrines and shrouds of darkness. It is the grandest opportunity. To journey this way is to meet the God inside and deny or embrace Her fully.

God has become my lover.
It is so much more than sex.

She spent her mornings riding the dawn with God.
Somewhere out of the early darkness,
    I would call to her.
And this calling lifted me out of my beliefs and into
            my knowing self.
Day after day, I would rush into her arms.
She would take me into herself
and set me down at the feet of Love.
We would reside there, watching the sun pass,
    watching our lives pass, like grapes to our lips.
Now I spend my mornings riding the dawn with God.
Somewhere out of the darkness,
        she calls to me, and I, in turn,
            set my daily compass to her star.

We did not come here to play small.

Do not grovel before God and beg God's forgiveness. God does not forgive. From that divine vantage point, there is <u>nothing</u> to forgive! Forgiveness is what returns us from an illusion of separateness. God isn't the one hanging out in that false premise. God is never separate from us. We push God away by believing we are not worthy. Forgive yourself. Know yourself. Return to Love.

We strive for perfection fearing the consequences of a wrong decision.

How exhausting!

Choosing to put love first, our psyches relax. There is no wrong move! The mental mud settles and what works best moment-to-moment becomes undoubtedly clear. No angst. No regret. No floundering. No separateness. No drama! Just love.

Simple.

When you decide that worry is no longer an option, love wells up in you and the rest appears to just take care of itself! You will be getting things done seemingly without effort. The spirit of Love in you will be providing you with all the abundant energy you require.

The beauty of walking through life with an illness like mine is that it keeps me honest with myself. There is no room for judgment, resistance, or being inauthentic. On the other hand, love is the great healer. I fly on love with no wings. I live a life of health and energy even when diseased.

We fly together, you and I,
when your mind is not looking.

Awaken to your body as the Christ that came to both live and then die into the Spirit's final knowing of itself. No need to improve the beauty that God placed into a heart which in turn, like a potter, devotedly fashioned into its own bowl special lines and curves, divots and weaves that speak of only you. Know your divinity! When fingers touch and lips caress, let them be the fingers and lips that love themselves, the ones that know no shame, that seek no improvement of what is already exalted blood and bone. Teach them to claim their completeness, their perfection as they are, vehicles of love, messengers of gratitude for the brief and precious life given them. Let them sing with their touch their most self-embracing songs. Let yourself know the Godly experience of soul and flesh made whole.

It's amazing the way life works, the opportunities that arise in their own time, synchronized with our willingness to grow. My freedom is here, now, in this fresh new breath that carries no stale air of past times. I stay here and I win the game. The game of peace.

I linger here to be a balm for the wounded,
to point towards the meeting place
of all souls.

Why do you linger?

Everywhere I go I am in my classroom. I am a teacher. I teach through being. And so, my friend, aware of it or not, are you.

God, I am in your blessed hands.
Tell me your dreams.
I will make them come true.

The universe is personal.
It is also extremely impersonal.

Embracing that contradiction is the key.
It is what keeps us humble and connected,
soul to soul.

.

When I speak the word of Love to friends, when I live the song of elation that we are, so many respond with reservation or even anger that I am reminded just how much of life's magic we shroud with misunderstanding. When I am sharing this joy that is our birthright and I am greeted like an unwelcome stranger, I am shown where the confusion lies, that you do not recognize the God in me as your own. Call it anything you want, the same essence enlivens us both. Only fear confuses this issue, fear of foolishness, fear of doctrine, fear of not being enough, fear of sin, of losing control.... All of these the many arguments we use to destroy our happiness...and our togetherness no less.

There is no use in hate.
Retribution tears at the fabric of our sanity,
no matter how seemingly justifiable.

Stand for what you know works.
Do it lovingly.

Obsession is a form of opium. Days upon days of distraction. Our minds long to forget how much they miss peace while refusing at the very same time to simply claim it.

I personally would rather be an obedient servant to Love.

God, my heart has been wrung out, dried,
and then soaked in the essence of You.

Wake up!!!!!
Joy is all that awaits you.
It smiles curiously at your mind,
            incomprehensible moron,
                    ol' trickster,
                        meanie.
Our minds can be monstrous.....
            and oh, so ridiculously lovable.

The untamed mind will abandon you.

Thank God there is a way of producing wings of our own internal creation. I can be inside this experience of Lyme disease and lay down overtones of liberation nonetheless. If breathing in and out in prayer is all I can do for this moment, it is gift enough to myself and this world. Accepting and experiencing my multi-dimensionality is the way I exemplify what is possible.

God's body is vast.
I have lost track,
becoming so attentive to a line on His hand that
traces the shape of you,
I have forgotten all the rest.
You have become my surroundings.
Savoring,
I curl into this crevasse that reaches out
and contains me.
For the time being, it is all there is, all I
perceive there to be.
That hand will reach away to embolden
something else.
It is bound away, lovingly,
to reveal the Greater Self.
It is then that I will climb to the nape of His
neck
and slide behind His eyes.
I will merge with His vision and
become His heart,
carrier of riches, oxygen and nutrients
to you, dear one,
and your specific holy land
upon God's body
that I once called home.

Hello, My Beloved Moon.
You've followed me so diligently,
so patiently around every corner.
You've met me quietly at all my dead ends.
You constantly reflect my light back to me.
Together, we trace tender fingers across the sky.
I am erratic fire.
You are elegantly honed surrender.
My soul wanders &
you are the expression of that soul
imbued with Godliness.
I forget, my Love, so often,
and you are my perfect Reminder.
Moon.

The eyes of a teacher can dig caverns into the soul &
fill them up with learning.
They can hold standards up like a prayer,
like a sacredness not to be diminished by thoughts of
mediocrity.
Stillness is a teacher calling out.
It quells the doubt and demands new and potent
action always here and
Now... Now...Now!
Spirit is a teacher that speaks the hardest truth with
the kindest voice.
The ears of a teacher take their direction from God
within.
The heart of a teacher seeps love and teaches by
blending fearlessly with its other.

I sought to keep close to me
the most precious thing of all.
And then God whispered,
"My Sweet Love,
That is not for you to keep.
Give. Give it away."

Your hands are the gifts through which God sings some of Her sweetest songs. The power of touch is a force that heals or harms.

Let's reach out towards each other and not cease until our touch reaches the furthest corners of each other's beings, wraps around them and makes them laugh. I want zero separation. Utter union has rooms with open windows and no doors between them. Then we will taste the love we've yearned for all our lives, the one that digs in deep and pulls one soul up from deep inside the other.

You have turned me into springtime. These words are flowers emerging everywhere. They astound the ground. In fall, leaves were littered across layers of summer's leftover treasures. Golden turned grey and winter stripped me bare of memory. So deepened into cold, I nearly forgot myself. I emptied out my pockets for the sake of abstinence. Nothing grew, only rested, as all things must in their time. That was before your arrival. Now the glorious emerges from its slumber and ignites in me my reverence for the Love that has arrived and brought this new period, this new and emboldened laughter with Her. Your eyes are suns that burn their poetry into my inner soil and awaken all the fertile seeds. They are sprouting into their impassioned destinies.

You have become as I am becoming, examples of different phases of the same transformation, a living how-to manual with pictures of the process and its final outcome. You've inhaled. I am still inhaling. Together, we elicit hope. Together, we leave room for not one excuse. Joy is achievable. Being big is a choice. It's a viable alternative to going back to sleep.

I have made a study of love, what it means to be it actually, fully, without exception. It is my 24/7 job and I am so grateful to have chosen it.

The option to self-destruct is always present. It whispers with the breath I give it. It is not real, though it claims to be. It is only a choice that I've given life to over and over so that it has grown a seemingly solid self. It's become my default. That is all. So it takes consciousness to shift that. I am not my father, my mother. Like fears, their ways are familiar, something I fall back on. I didn't come here to fall back. I came here to sit still, tall and strong, not to be swayed or laid down. I'm here to evolve.

I can't be God in other people's lives,
only in my own.

When I choose, as I have in so many moments,
to confuse my ego with God -- Ha! Not to worry!
There is always a tremendously painful scrape or burn
written into the contract of that decision.

151

Some worry about becoming arrogant
if they taste the elixir of true confidence.

God is too wise to ever let the insecurity that belies
arrogance be a comfortable or authentically happy
place to live.

Humility, on the other hand,
is willing to look however it must,
foolish, arrogant, stubborn, or otherwise,
in order to serve Love.

Rejecting yourself never works. Never.

Living a life of love does not necessarily mean living easy. It always means living peacefully. What hard work it is to learn to relax! May we know it as our primary task, worthy of our full-time employment.

I've been getting lost in God's garden for longer and longer periods these days. I choose to enter and the scents and sounds unravel me. My orientation shifts. I no longer know the direction back to the moment before I came to be here now nor would I want to. I've finally released the drugs and addictions that bound me to the world. It is a most delicious alteration, this emerging landscape that has always awaited me so patiently within. I recommend it to everyone.

I want you to learn to reach deep inside my chest, wrap your fingers around my heart and know it as your own. There is nothing there to distrust, nothing to wonder about, no fear or doubt of us. Only light and God's breath live in this chamber singing beloved songs to each other that all begin with your name.

There is no sunrise I'd rather come to know
than the one that wakes me again to your eyes.

This world is a place where we either make our stand for love or we go down with the ship, the ship of indecision, the ship of self-rejection, the ship of doubt, the ship of suspicion. These are all the same titanic....sinking.

You are my mind's most exotic flavor. The lip and the caress. Softened skin of ripened fruit. Iridescent eyes and the molded rounded word. The way the flame can light the tinder. The way a road can curve suddenly and spill itself upon a vista. You are a pronouncement so prophetic none of us gets it, not even you. My entire body responds to this message. It is the call I hear and know and yet must patiently await its own remembrance. The task of non-action as I bear witness to your awakening is the hardest, most alluring I've known.

I know that I called this pain to me like the stone calls to the chisel, like the prairie calls to the flame, the wildfire that ensures its natural ecological cycle, cleansing and enriching itself to begin again. This pain is my chosen destiny. To be carved out, hollowed and molded, scorched if need be, by God's artistic touch, carving the illusory away to lay my soul bare, unveiled, open to all things of this world. Free. A container of light. A usable gift. A blessing. A friend.

Pain is the great teacher of compassion.

Let it deepen you.

Secretly, the generosity that I exhibit is who you long to be. It's why your mind hates me. It's why you want me.

You seek to serve two masters.
That will never do.
Only Love, my dear, only Love will satisfy.

My mind doesn't have a clue what love is. It thinks it does but then seeks to box it in with walls of rules and limitations, always an attempt to keep itself safe. My heart sits back effortless and marveling. It knows everything about love and, loving, doesn't mind the misunderstanding. It doesn't mind anything at all.

I always want to be on the frontlines
of the greatest need.

I woke you with trepidation, like a child, gingerly, a first attempt, awkward, wary. I woke you blindfolded, at once confident then doubtful, a sea-saw between worlds of love and worlds of fear. My purpose clear, then not. Desire pulling me towards the bed alongside you to swoon in delusional slumber and feel the bodies' blended warmth, a tempting consolation. Hesitation aside, I did in fact wake you though with a half-heartedness that did not inspire the joy in you to emerge lightly into the world. Don't let my approach deter you from its deeper meaning. Make up your own morning from here. Leave me behind if you must. Rise into this new day that is your life. It is the gift you deserve.

Under a façade of high-rolling endeavors, an air of strength, lions and diamonds intermixed, under the rough-edged instinct to survive, endure, and push away from pain, there is a softness inside you that speaks with an angel's voice. She is so tender. She has long fingers that trace the lines of rivers and earth that are this world, lovingly, with raw care. She longs to be heard. She waits patiently to speak.

I am the surgeon that brings a knife to cut through ego layers that surround the heart's truest expressions of itself. It will only hurt more if you twist and try to get away. After all, you begged for me to come. You begged on knees bended and kissing God's face for me to assist you. You told me to cut through no matter how you might show up in protest. Was it so long ago that you've forgotten? Lean in and hear the echoed whispers of the plan we made from the beginning, that you would let go of your deepest Self and I, with a knife, would inspire Her reclamation. No words of sweet longing from your mouth or mine will distract me from this promise. The soul's longing inside both of us is far stronger, far greater. It speaks to us. It calls us home.

Sometimes the greatest gift Love gives
is to crack the shell.

You are the road I will have looked down as far as possible and not taken. You will have been the greatest cost, the one I wanted with every cell and couldn't have had without betraying my promises to the Soul in you. A life beside you was the dream I held loosely for Love. No addiction to form will I allow to come between us. I gave you to God and now find you everywhere, inner, outer, no past, no future, always and increasingly us.

When I look into the world,
I see you without a face.

"What doesn't kill you makes you stronger."

Stronger in what way though?
In hate? In forgiveness? In vengeance?
In dignity? In self-destruction? In faith?

If you let it, what doesn't kill you can make you
stronger in love.

What are you strengthening inside yourself?

Love of the Spirit is the answer in all things.
The rest degrades,
slowly or quickly,
into worldly madness.

I came to awaken something inside you. Only the purest kind of love would do. I did awaken that something. I did reach in and hold your sacred wounded heart and remind it of its life and its purpose. No matter the path of in-loveness, it belongs to God and it is always true to its origin. Any other path is the mind's lesser version of the real deal.

I keep getting caught in the crossfire of your mind and heart opposing one another. The lasting ceasefire will only come when the mind finally surrenders to knowing that only the heart wins, only the heart can weave the magic robe that encompasses, only the heart loves, constant and sure, every single time. Your mind sees me as an angel, then the devil, depending on its tidal moods. Your heart knows me simply as another version of itself, capable of all things and precious as it gets, journeying the great River, always us.

I have a dream for us that is beyond all apparent possibility. It is a dream not born of this world or the limits of our minds. I must give this dream a life here on this plane, even without your cooperation, without your faith in our love. I will put my blindfold on and mark this road with footsteps guided by the inner light that calls me towards you across shadowy passes through darkened doubt. If I hold true, perhaps I can awaken you. If I hold strong, perhaps I can help you to move the mountain that is your mind. Rekindling my joy for this process that is my life, the daily act of creating sweet wonder out of things entirely intangible, perhaps we will one day be whole again. I better get to work....

I come here to swim in my own bath of love that I steep you in every day from across the miles. I come to immerse myself in my Self, to get as close as I can to this incredible contact that is ours. You will not let me in so I don't invite myself. Still, I hover at the edges of you and gaze inward. The love that is in me for you gives birth to stars. It is a generator of goodness in me. You are a flower my mind will not be rid of. Your soul is my heart's desire.

There is a luscious soft place in you. I remember that room. I don't quite know how I entered. It was beyond the mind. The guards must have been asleep that night. Now they know better and have doubled their locks and bars. I know of no way in anymore. I've stopped watching for their slumber. Until you release them of their vigil, they will stake their righteous claim as protectors of a garden even you no longer remember is there.

One day,
to your great surprise,
you are going to discover
that every move I have ever made
has been replete with your design.

We don't attribute consciousness to our organs in part because we focus so much on the physical chemistry of these parts of ourselves. At the same time, can you view the consciousness of the brain under a microscope? Not yet. We can witness neurons firing in response to thoughts/emotions. That's as close as we've yet come to documenting consciousness. Are there not endless neurons throughout the body as there are inside the brain? What is the difference between these? We need to give more credence to the unique consciousness of each organ, the wisdom it contributes physically as well as emotionally, mentally, and on all levels. We need to listen to them speak of the challenges they've inherited and are seeking to mend. Each organ has its own process of evolution, which supports the evolution of the whole. When we feed our bodies pure food, it supports clean emotion and clear thinking in that organ. It allows that organ to work harmoniously which helps the whole. The layers of us-ness are cellular, systemic, familial, and societal, all in ways that mirror and integrate one another. Our responsibility in this evolution has become evident.

Love knows no boundaries, no limitations.

Then what is this insanity of being human,
this expanse of loss and grief?
It is the great misconception.
It is the kiln's fire.

True love can <u>only</u> emerge
in the letting go of fear.

There are times
        the moth doesn't want to
                burn.
The flames seem instead to
        be chasing us into
                every unavoidable turn.
When we finally realize that
        it is our souls that are
                that fire,
        hunting us for our own sakes,
                we will enter willingly
        the transmutation into light
                that is our calling, our destiny,
                        our birthright.

Where are you?
Where did you go, my dear soul friend? We met in God's river. I will not forget. We could stop all of this crazy talk and re-immerse. It is hard to let go of that moment. It is gone though. It is rotting in my system because I have refused to digest it. It was glorious. So glorious to see us both take all of the masks and filters off to be in raw nakedness together. It was real and I won't forget it though I will release it into what is no longer here. It was and now it is not. You are no longer with me at God's table. I will sit down to eat even if alone. God bless you as you go. God bless us all as we walk along this road, this path of learning to let things be as they are.

I cracked my heart open against your stone
and God's light came pouring out.

What you call love doesn't feel like love to me. It feels heavy and judgmental, needy and obsessive. It feels imprisoning and unkind and dangerous. It feels treacherous and self-involved. It feels like it will lash out at me any minute with its vengeance. It won't be there for me in times of trouble because it is seeking its own fulfillment in me and when I don't have it to give, it gets angry instead of compassionate. Forgive me if I don't care to move towards that. Addictive love is not love at all. It carries swords and sticks them into itself saying that I am the abuser. No more. No more. No more.

Why would you settle for the crumbs from one human's table when you have the creator of the universe offering you limitless love?

It is challenging to live a truly honest life. Humility is inevitably necessary for this. We want so very many things in life that we are unwilling to pay the cost for. We want to be healthy, but we don't want to have to change our diets. We want to be loved, meanwhile we don't want to face our demons, the parts we don't like in us. We want security, but we don't want to do the work to build it inside of ourselves. So we look for it in others.

What a fruitless and dangerous game that is.

Nothing will keep me from loving you.
So sue me, kill me, beat me, retreat from me.
I love you, I love you, I love you.
My love is a river through the trees.
It is a sprouting from the cooled lava field.
It is a child in a nuclear winter.

No question about it.
I am absolutely out to manipulate you with my love.
I am out to seduce the passionate in you to awaken,
to look into its own reflection and love what it sees.
Sounds simple.
But it takes extreme measures oftentimes.
It takes uninhibited bravery on both our parts.
Cooperation.
Whether you somehow find that threatening
or not,
now that part is up to you.
What you do with the love I offer you
is entirely out of my control.

This time,
you have chosen to fashion out of the love I gave you
a gleaming knife,
threatening to wound yourself
with this homemade weapon.
At this point,
my love no longer resembles the gift
I had originally offered.
It has been mutilated with misunderstanding
beyond anything familiar.
There is a certain point,
whether I like it or not,
when I am cued to exit.
There's no use in
fueling destructive fires.
I withdraw the force you have turned me into
as a necessary response
to your ever-solidifying justification to fear.
The real you is no longer your desire.
Only a lonely tempestuous season
will satisfy you, or seem to, now.
I don't recognize who you've become.
I longed to warm your hearth with my tinder.
I wish you had allowed that with your trust.
I wish that so much.

It's strange.
As inner cities burn,
buildings and landscapes built with excruciating care,
hours of tender deliberations,
so many plans, dreams,
my precious own,
as my mind grieves, experiencing death,
my heart is here, trusting.
It is faithful,
even as it watches our gardens of ego cinder,
knowing, awaiting something more.
True love endures all things.
Loss is detoxifying.
It hurts so much.
And that burning is an opening up.

I have been cleansed by white flames of fear,
reduced to ash.
Rebuild me, Potter.
I give myself over to your innate sense of color
and steady hand.

I know now that Judas was Jesus' beloved friend and helper, not consciously per se, but on a soul level. To have done the reviling thing, that which would give Jesus his moment to rise up and exemplify love in spite of it ALL... He could not have done this without him.

Every single person in this world is either love or love disguised as fear.

From the words of the great master,
pray for those who persecute you.
Honor them.
They are helping you grow into your Spirit.

Unwind into the night. Come to me and lay your spirit in my center. Release fully. We are flying now. No hindrance. Our minds chains that we've turned to wings. An adventure. We hurl ourselves into realms of color, harmonics. We explore unknowns together.

You hate me in the day. You shun me. At night, while the mind sleeps, our spirits flirt fearlessly. At night, we lean dynamically into forever. We fly across the sky. We bless the world with our eternal love.
You and I.

I would die for you
and I mean it.
I just won't help you
drown.

Rise like a phoenix
from your deepest disappointments.
You can.

Will you?

The next true revolution will be an inner one,
stepping beyond our self-made cages,
the remaining frontier.

When your heart gets a notion to do something,
do it quick
before your mind,
party-pooper that it can be,
starts in.

It is a magi's trick how the mind can twist the magnificent mechanics of this human experience, this tactile world, into something it labels 'boring.'

Let my love be a table at which you feast and yet do not linger. Do not be deterred by the radiance in my heart, for you have such glorious radiance to discover of your own, so many miles of sun-bathed dips and turns in the road of your soul. Rest for a moment here in my warmth and then move on. Without distraction, let your send-off be the song of God inside me, all praise. I'll sing you a farewell that will echo in the ear seeking comfort in the miles ahead. Your journey will be a blessed one. On it, we will be united, honoring God, as the compass turns us about in divergent directions. My compass takes me to the ground, so humbled by this heart of service, this absolute need for God within. When you seek me out again, get on your knees and hands, sink low into the dirt, and make a few soft sounds to call me out. I will arise from within so free and well-nourished, a devoted earthworm, tending effulgently to your inner soil.

I wish to give myself to my work as though with each effort I am bending to care for my Beloved. I will give energetically to Her each time I reach out to give of myself to another. I will steep the act of giving in my love for Her. And She and I and those with whom I exchange will be blessed in a magical and holy union by my continual remembrance and honoring of this devotion I carry. And our daughter, whose soul I embrace with my own each day as I dream and each night as I sleep, will be gifted with a subtle and powerful remembrance of her place in God's myriad things. She will know, at the precise time that she so desires it, that there are many thresholds awaiting her within her own heart and upon each is written, with her own empowered hand, the many names of Love.

I close this door, knowing there is no door. I release you, knowing I will never have to let you go. I survive this world by knowing it is not the real one. Love will return to itself. It is who we are. Surely as the sun returns, this love will remember itself again.

How many times have I leaned towards normalcy
when I came here to be extraordinary?

We come here to love and then we forget.

It is time now, Friend, to remember.

To all who have loved and supported me,
my endless gratitude.

Please contact the author with any questions or
comments or to order more copies of
Love Song.

hcybele@gmail.com

All proceeds from the sale of this book
will go towards
the alleviation of suffering.

Made in United States
Troutdale, OR
12/21/2023